CANADIAN POP & ROCK
SHEET MUSIC
PlayList

Arranged by Dan Coates

Flag: © istockphoto/Valerie Loiseleux

Alfred Publishing Co., Inc.
16320 Roscoe Blvd., Suite 100
P.O. Box 10003
Van Nuys, CA 91410-0003
alfred.com

WINTER GAMES

(1988 Winter Olympics Theme)

By David Foster
Arranged by Dan Coates

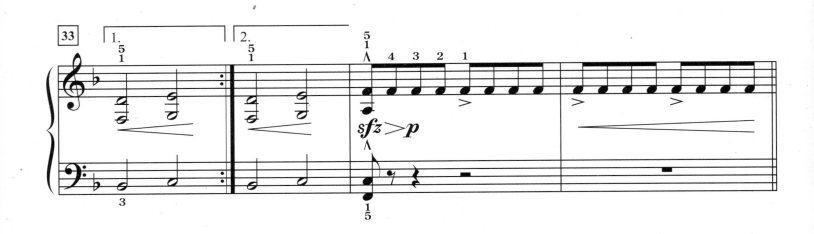

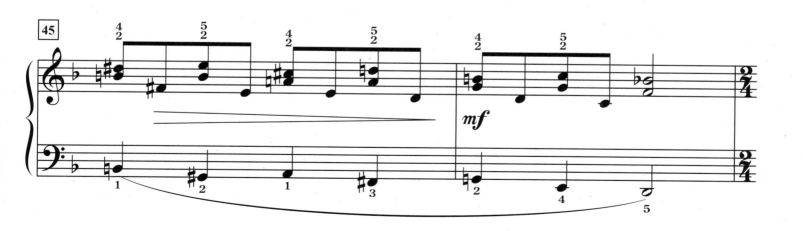

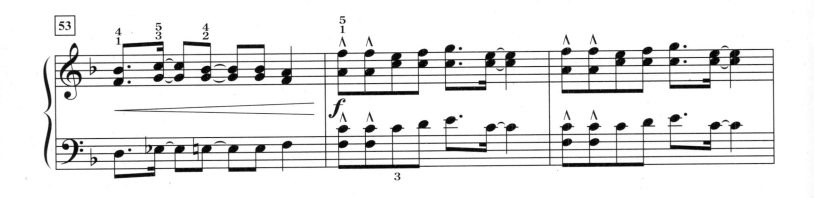

BECAUSE YOU LOVED ME

(Theme from "Up Close and Personal")

Words and Music by Diane Warren
Arranged by Dan Coates

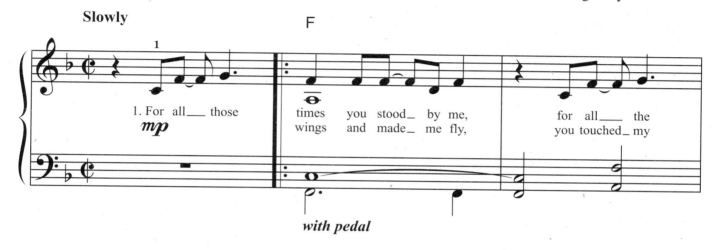

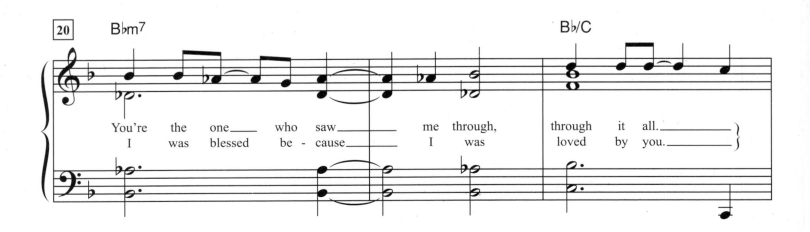

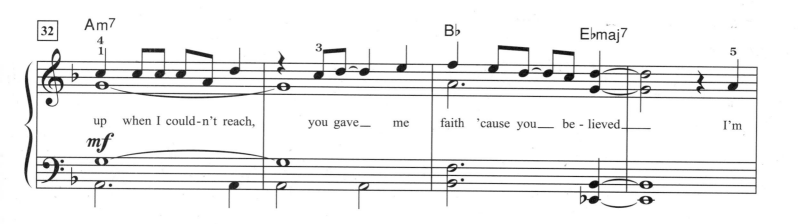

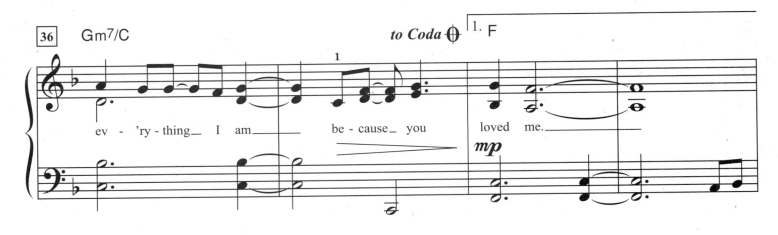

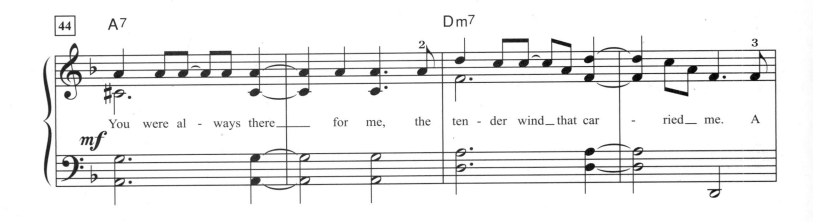

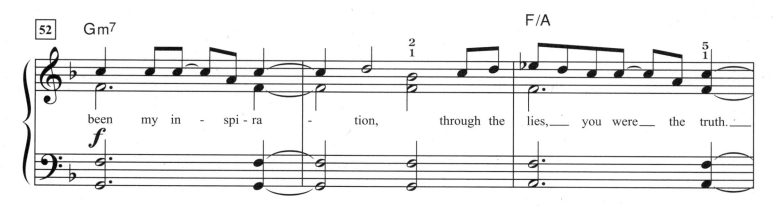

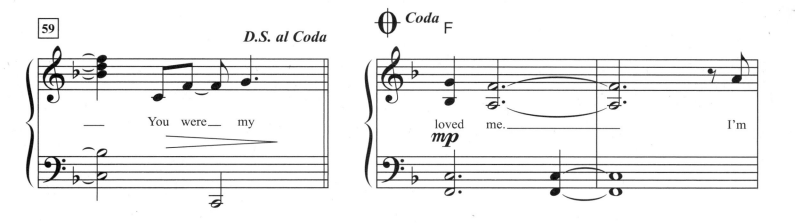

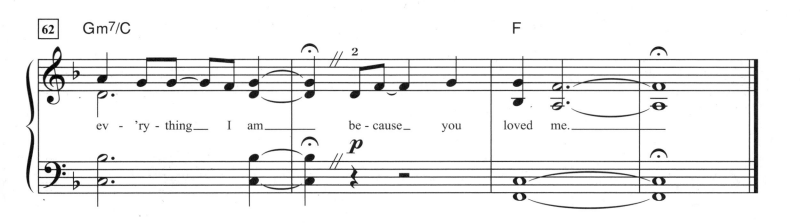

BELIEVE

(CTV Promotional Theme - Winter Olympics 2010)

By Howard Shore
Arranged by Dan Coates

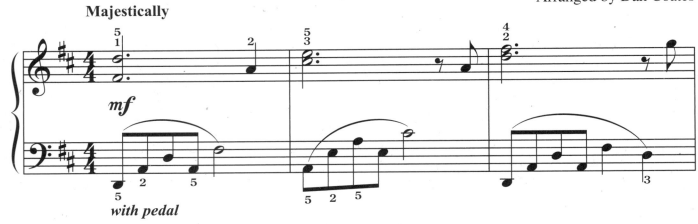

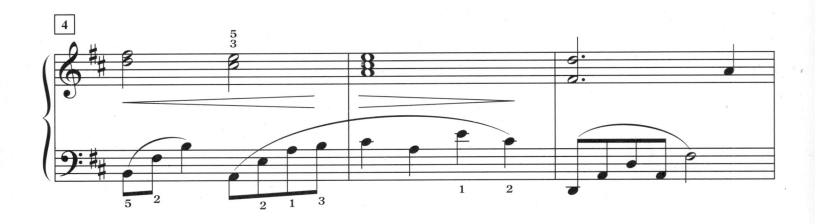

BIG YELLOW TAXI

Words and Music by Joni Mitchell
Arranged by Dan Coates

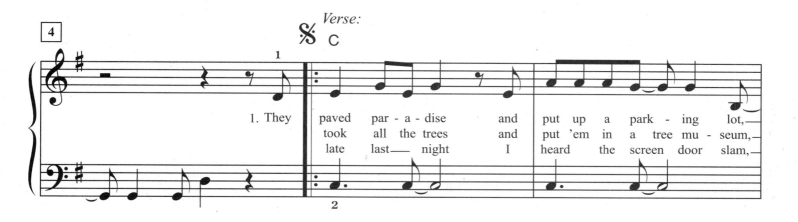

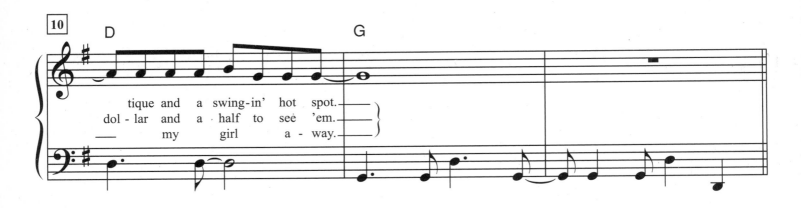

Bridge:

Ooh, _____ bop. _____ Hey, farm - er, farm - er, put

cresc. *f*

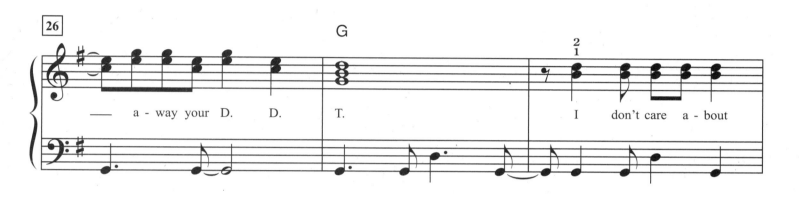

_____ a - way your D. D. T. I don't care a - bout

spots on my ap - ples, leave _____ me the birds and bees. _____

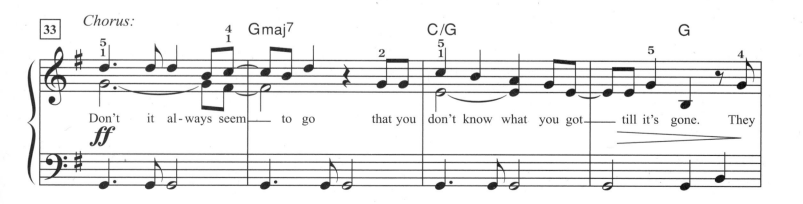

Chorus:

Don't it al - ways seem _____ to go that you don't know what you got _____ till it's gone. They

ff

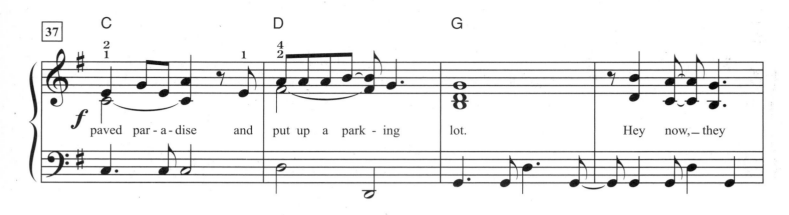

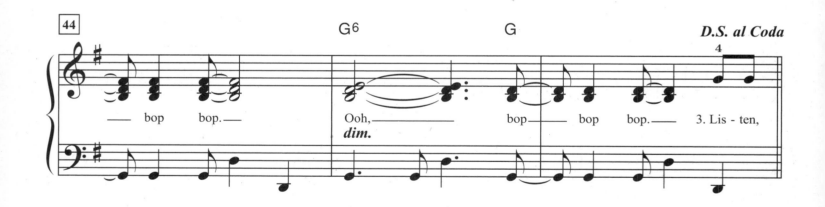

don't know what you got — till it's gone. They paved par-a-dise and put up a park-ing

lot. — Hey, — hey, hey. — They paved par-a-dise to put up a park-ing

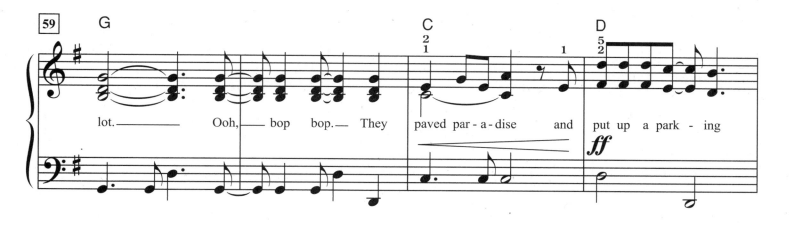

lot. — Ooh, — bop bop. — They paved par-a-dise and put up a park-ing

lot. —

COMPLICATED

Words and Music by
Lauren Christy, Graham Edwards,
Scott Spock and Avril Lavigne
Arranged by Dan Coates

Moderately slow rock, in 2

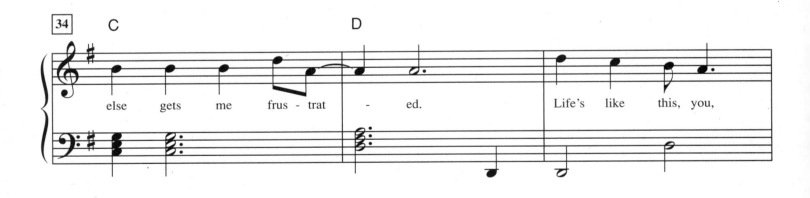

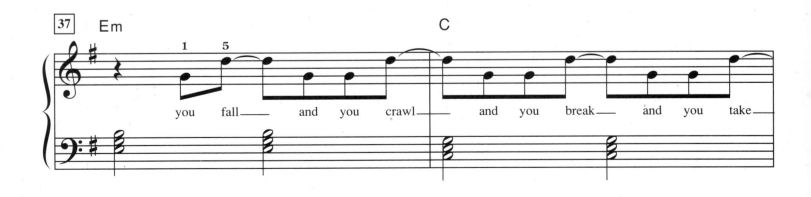

EVERYTHING

Words and Music by
Michael Bublé, Alan Chang And Amy Foster
Arranged by Dan Coates

Moderately, with a steady beat

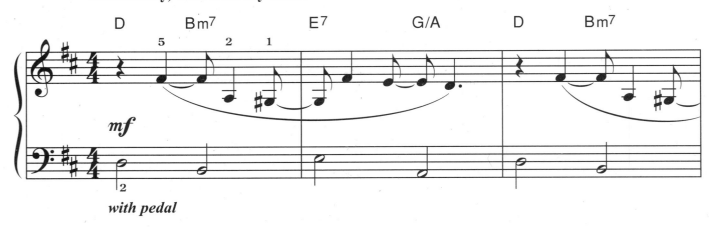

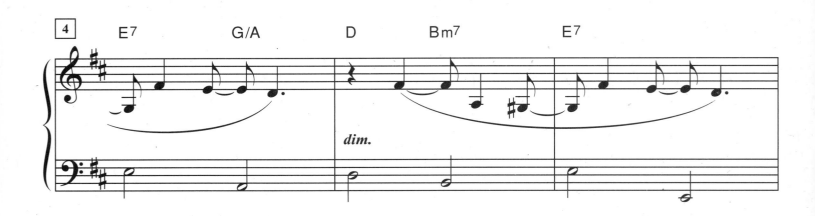

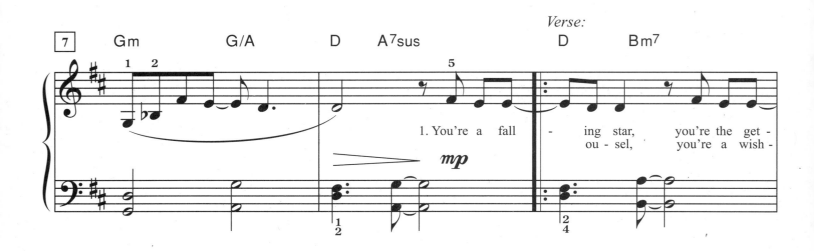

27

(EVERYTHING I DO) I DO IT FOR YOU

Words and Music by
Bryan Adams, Robert John "Mutt" Lange and Michael Kamen
Arranged by Dan Coates

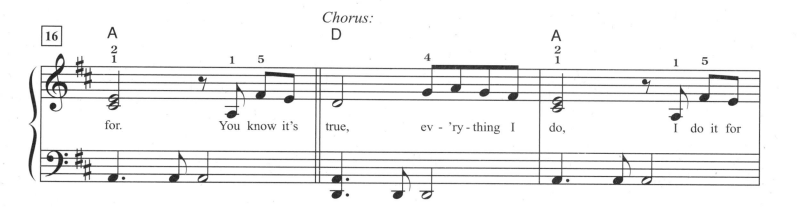

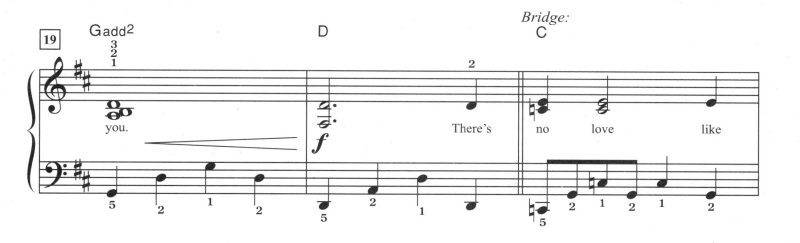

no way, un-less you're there all the time,_____ all the

way,_____ yeah.

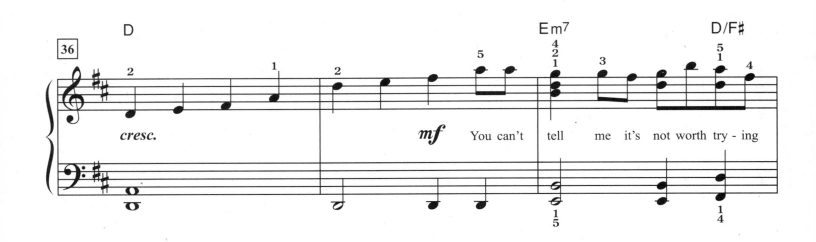

You can't tell me it's not worth try-ing

HAVE YOU EVER REALLY LOVED A WOMAN?

Music by Michael Kamen
Lyrics by Bryan Adams and Robert John "Mutt" Lange
Arranged by Dan Coates

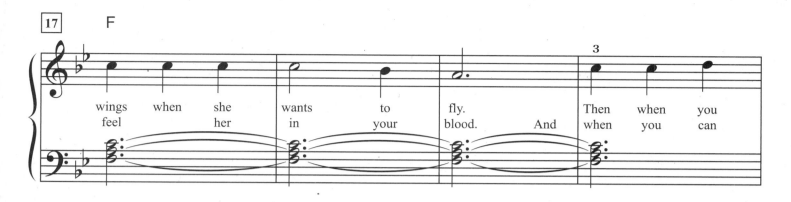

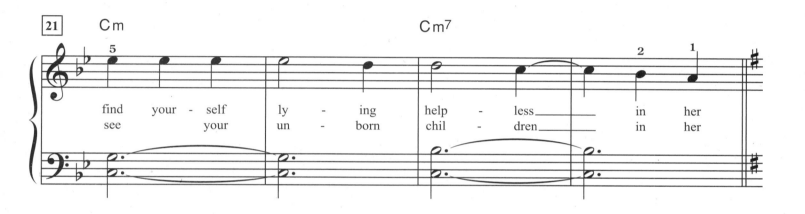

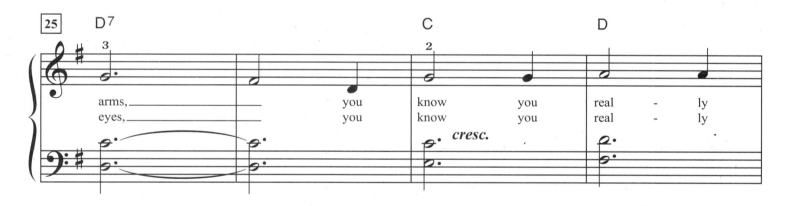

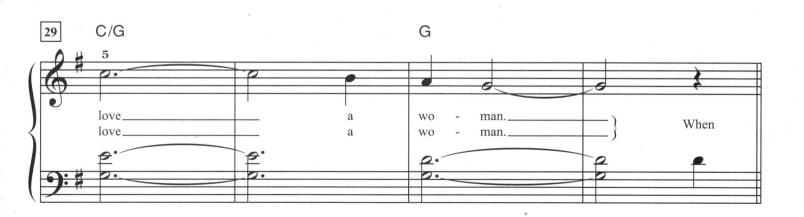

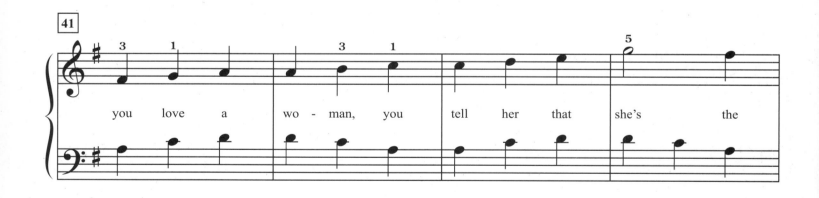

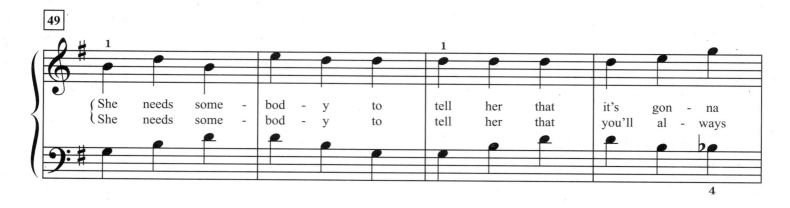

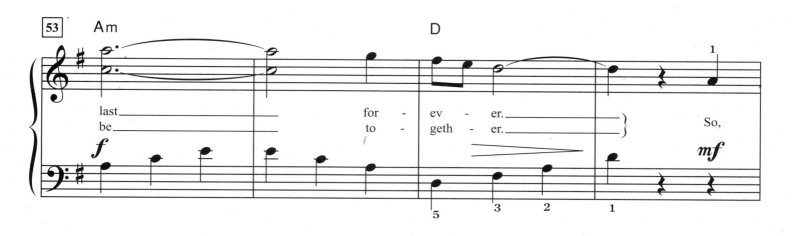

Chorus:

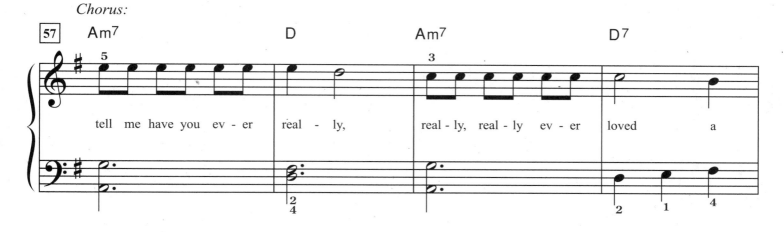

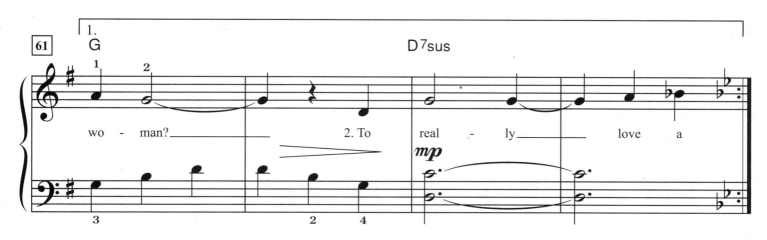

wo - man? _____ Just,

mf

tell me have you ev - er real - ly, real - ly, real - ly ev - er loved a

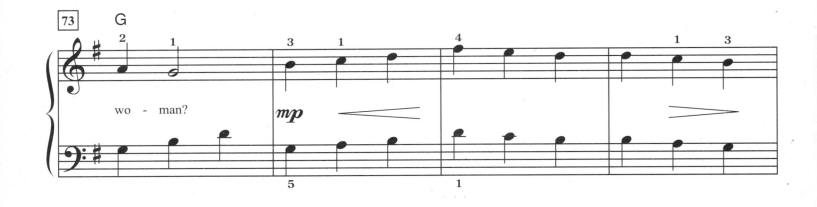

wo - man? *mp*

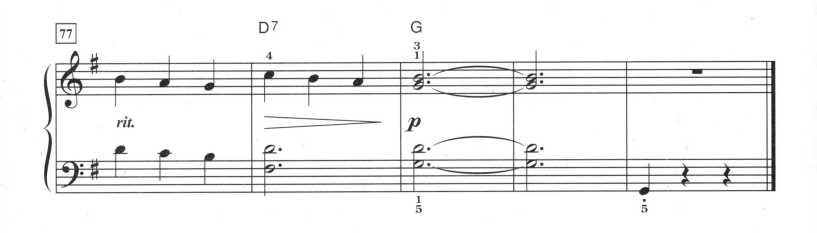

rit. *p*

HERO

(from "Spider-Man")

Words and Music by Chad Kroeger
Arranged by Dan Coates

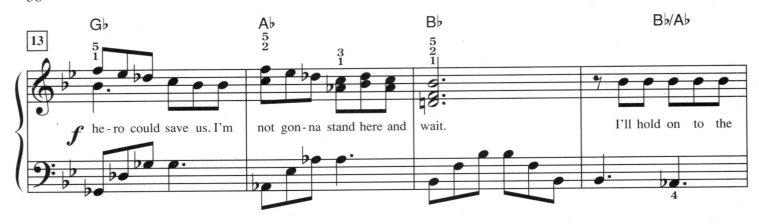

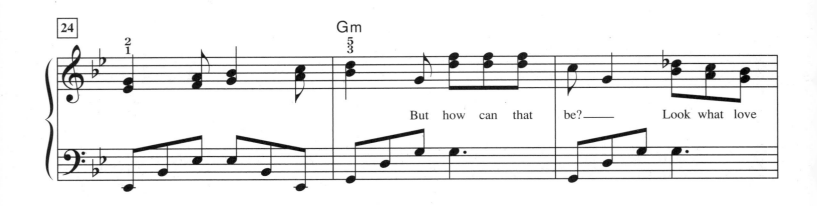

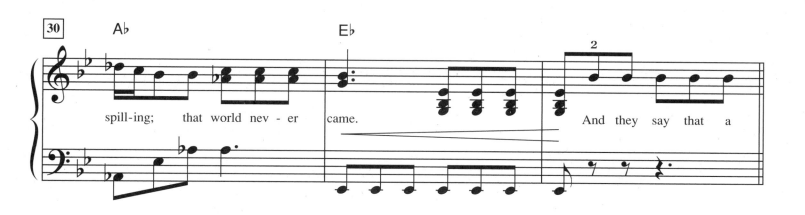

IF YOU ASKED ME TO

Words and Music by Diane Warren
Arranged by Dan Coates

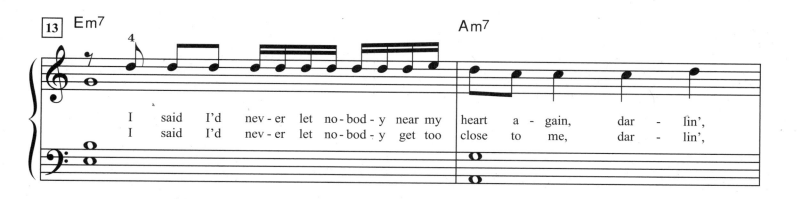

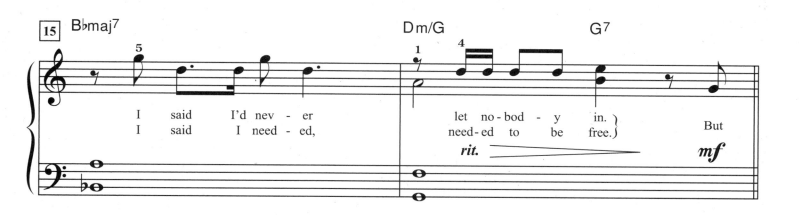

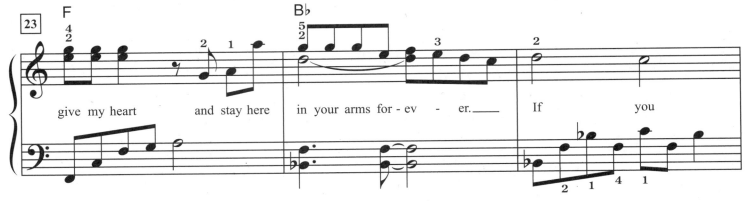

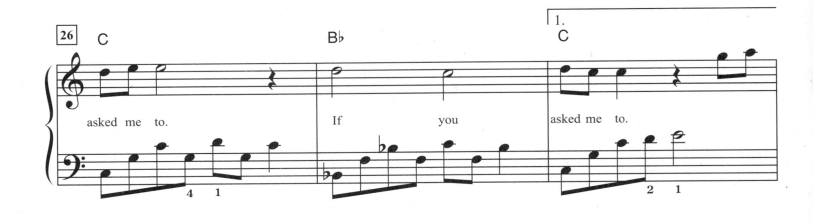

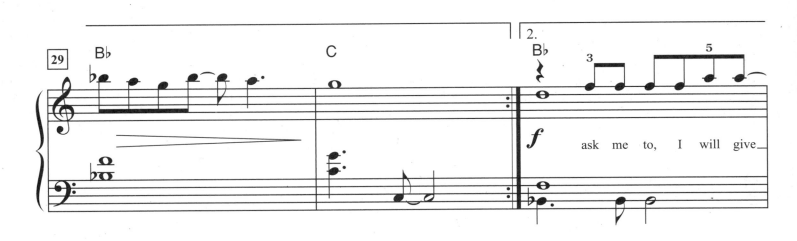

LOST

Words and Music by
Michael Bublé, Alan Chang And Jann Arden
Arranged by Dan Coates

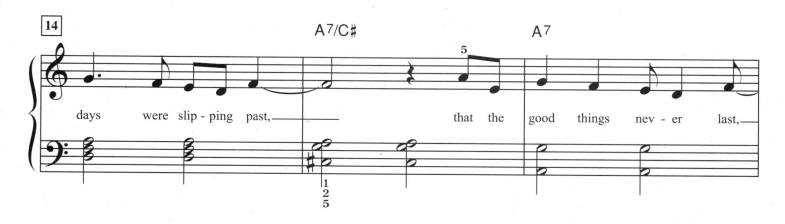

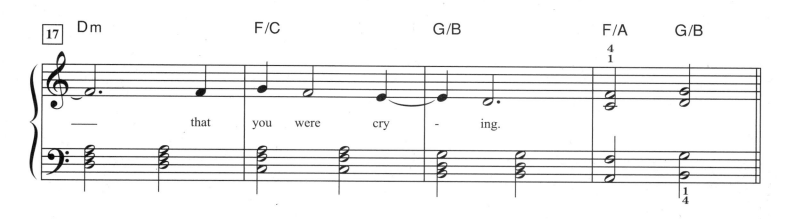

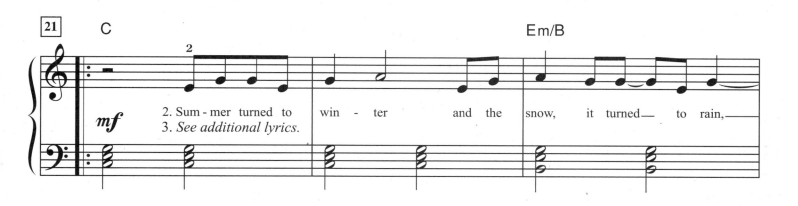

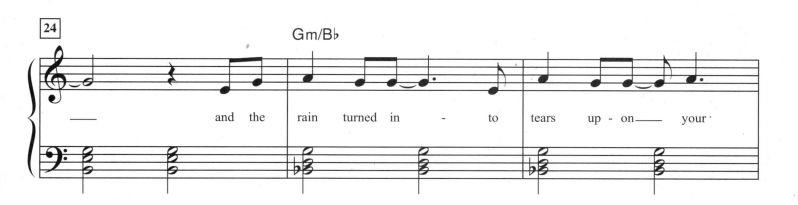

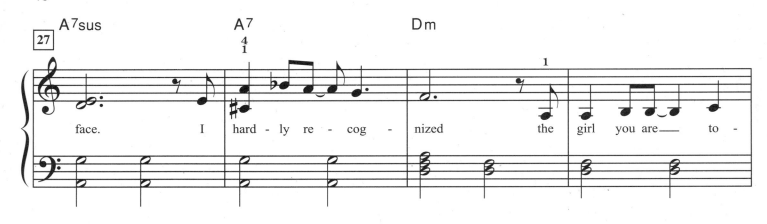

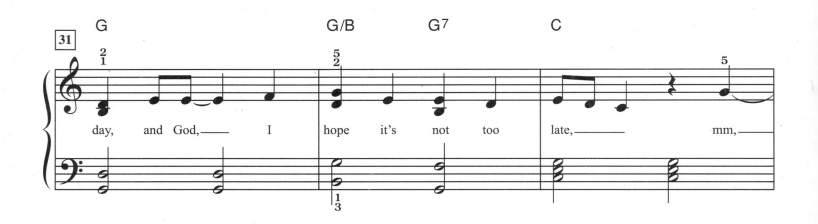

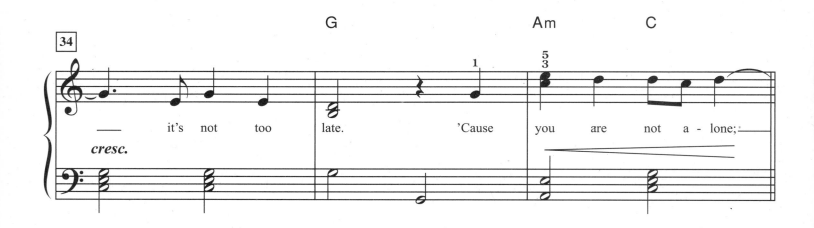

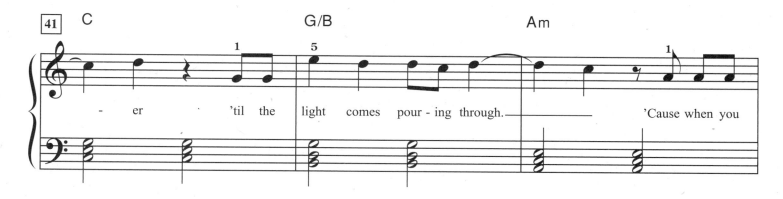

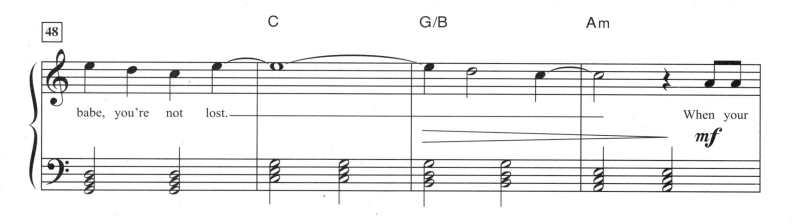

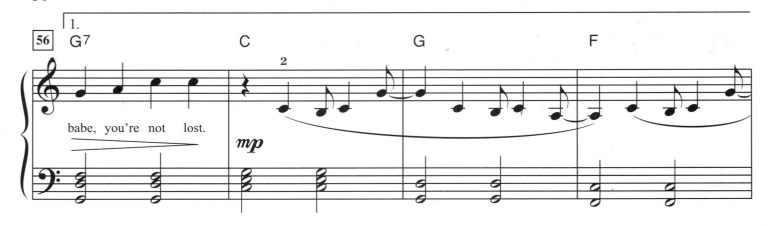

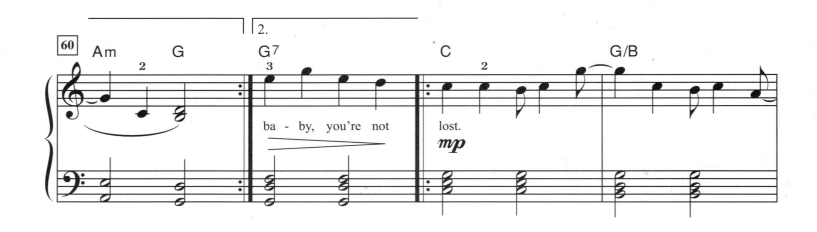

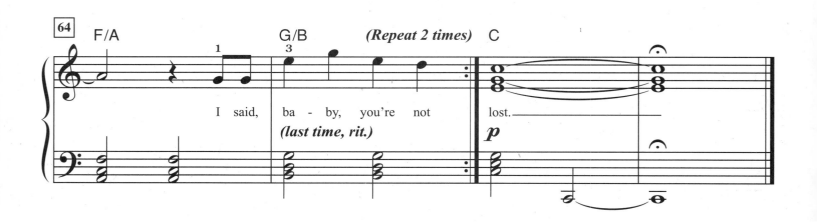

Verse 3:
Life can show no mercy;
It can tear your soul apart.
It can make you feel like you've gone crazy
But you're not.
Though things have seemed to change,
There's one thing that's the same.
In my heart you have remained
And we can fly, fly, fly away.
(To Chorus:)

THE NIGHT THEY DROVE OLD DIXIE DOWN

Words and Music by Robbie Robertson
Arranged by Dan Coates

13 Am   F   Am

hun - gry,_____ just___ bare - ly a - live._____ I took the train to

16 F   C   Am

Rich - mond that fell;_____ it was a time I re - mem - ber, oh,___ so___

Chorus:

19 D7   C

well._____ The night___ they

f

22 Am   F   C   Am

drove old Dix - ie down.____ And all the bells were ring - in' the

Verse 2:
Back with my wife in Tennessee,
And one day she said to me,
"Virgil, quick come see.
There goes the Robert E. Lee."
Now, I don't mind I'm choppin' wood,
And I don't care if my money's no good.
Just take what you need and leave the rest,
But they should never have taken the very best.
(To Chorus:)

Verse 3:
Like my father before me,
I'm a working man.
And like my brother before me,
I took a rebel stand.
Well, he was just eighteen, proud and brave,
But a Yankee laid him in his grave.
I swear by the blood below my feet,
You can't raise the Caine back up
When it's in defeat.
(To Chorus:)

PHOTOGRAPH

Lyrics by Chad Kroeger
Music by Nickelback
Arranged by Dan Coates

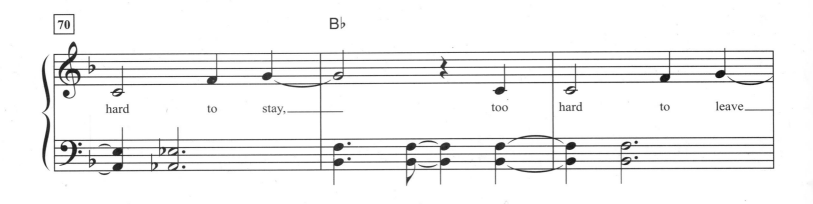

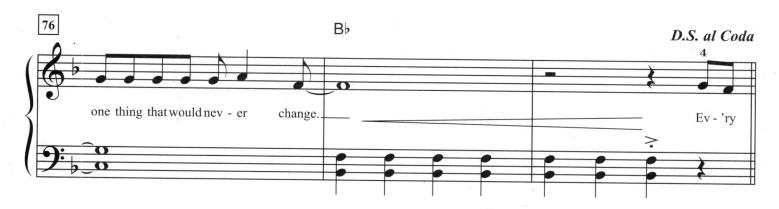

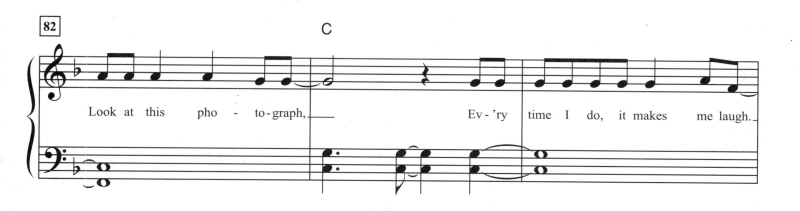

UNTITLED

(How Can This Happen to Me?)

Words and Music by Simple Plan
Arranged by Dan Coates

Moderately slow

Verse:

o - pen my eyes,— I try to see but I'm blind - ed by the white light.—

I can't re - mem - ber how,— I can't re - mem - ber why.— I'm

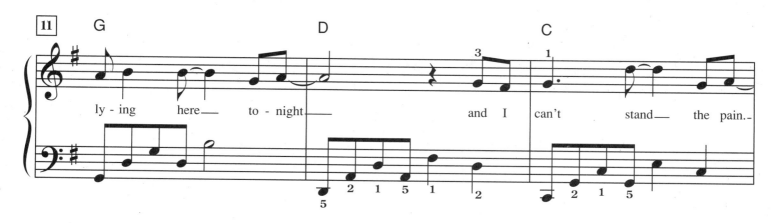

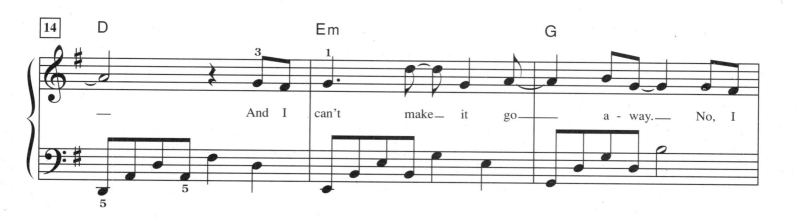

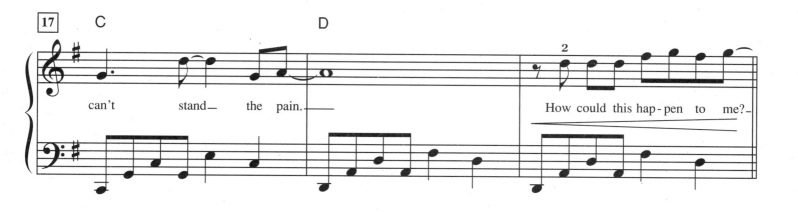

as I'm fad-ing a-way.___ I'm sick of this life,___ I just wan-na scream.

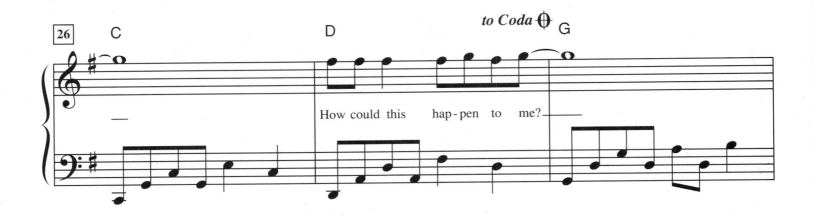

How could this hap-pen to me?___

Verse:

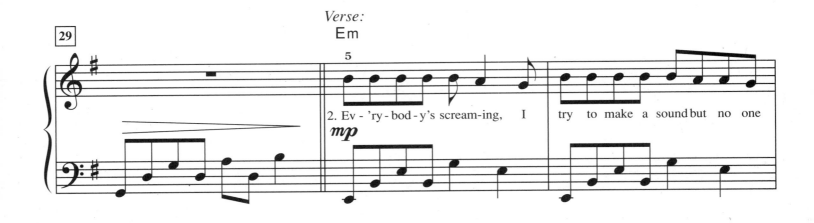

2. Ev-'ry-bod-y's scream-ing, I try to make a sound but no one

hears me.___ I'm slip-ping off the edge, I'm

35 hang-ing by a thread. I wan-na start this o-ver a-gain. So,

38 I try to hold on to a time when

41 noth-ing mat-tered and I can't ex-plain what hap-pened. And

44 I can't e-rase the things that I've done. *cresc.*

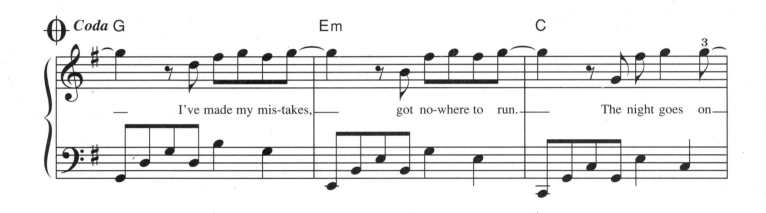

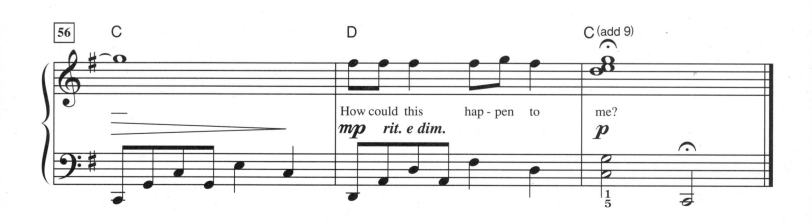

YOU NEEDED ME

Words and Music by Randy Goodrum
Arranged by Dan Coates

HAVEN'T MET YOU YET

Words and Music by
Michael Bublé, Alan Chang and Amy Foster
Arranged by Dan Coates

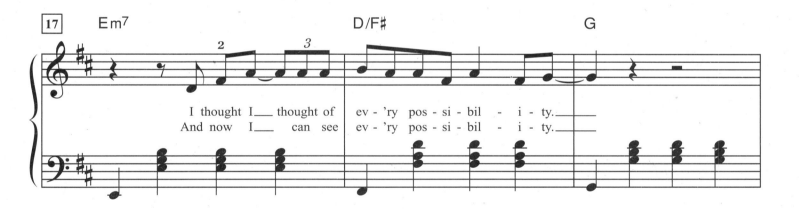

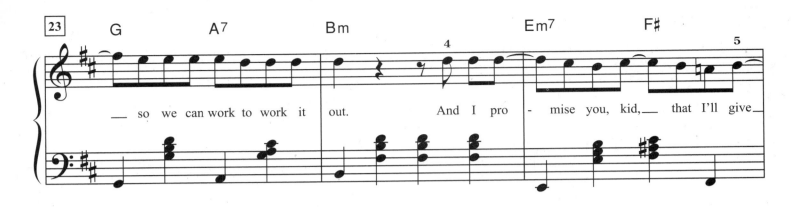

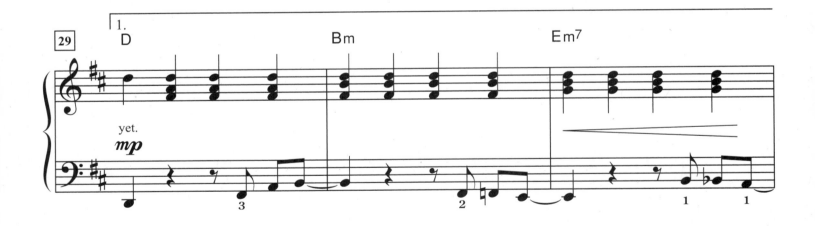

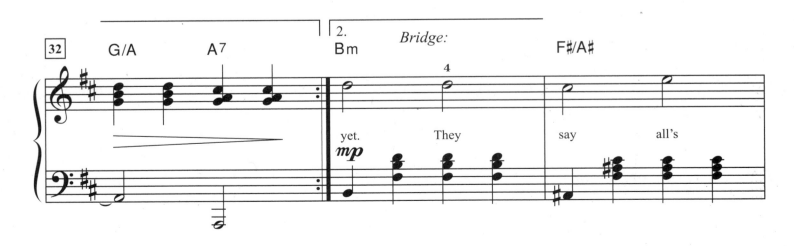

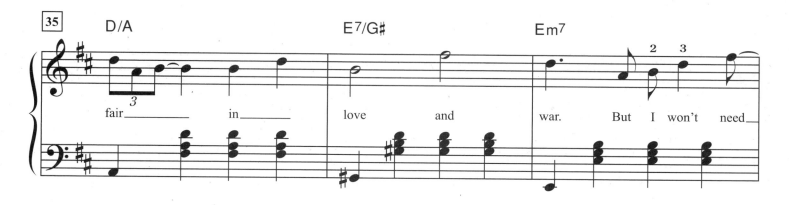

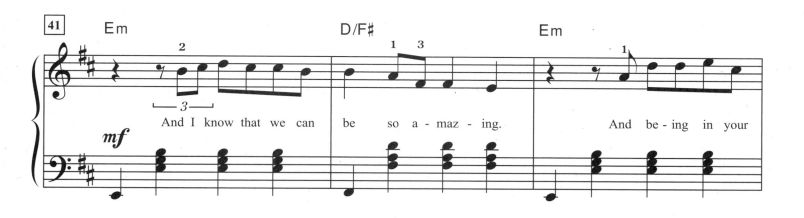

D.S. al Coda